Biology 3a — Life Processes

Pages 1-2 — Osmosis

Q1 a) side B
b) from B to A
c) The liquid level on side B will **fall**, because **water will flow from side B to side A by osmosis.**

Q2 a)

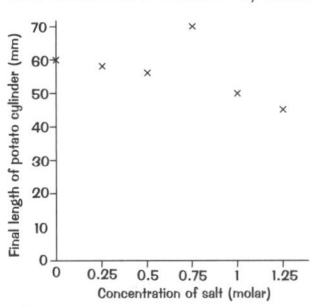

b)

Concentration of salt (molar)	Final length of potato cylinder (mm)	Change in length of potato cylinder (mm)
0	60	+10
0.25	58	+8
0.5	56	+6
0.75	70	+20
1	50	0
1.25	45	-5

c) i) 0.75 molar (it doesn't follow the pattern)
ii) Repeat the experiment at least twice more to find the most likely values.
d) Any three from, e.g: the volume of solution / the length of time the cylinders are left for / the surface area of the cylinders / the temperature.

Q3 a) tissue fluid
b) Water will move by osmosis from the tissue fluid into the body cells as the tissue fluid has a higher water concentration and the body cells have a lower water concentration.
c) The net movement of water molecules stops when there is an equal concentration of water molecules on either side of the membrane — when they have reached equilibrium.

Q4 a) Water molecules moved by osmosis from the pot (where they were in a higher concentration) to the meat (where they were in a lower concentration), thus adding size to the meat.
b) i) water / sugar solution
ii) It has come from inside the fruit by osmosis (to an area of lower water concentration where the sugar surrounds the fruit).
iii) The higher water concentration surrounding the fruit causes the movement of water from around the fruit to inside the fruit. This increases mass and makes the raisins and sultanas bigger.

Pages 3-4 — Gas and Solute Exchange

Q1 a)

Feature	Diffusion	Osmosis	Active transport
Substances move from areas of higher concentration to areas of lower concentration	✓	✓	
Requires energy			✓

b) Osmosis involves the movement of **water.**
Q2 a) True
b) True
c) False
d) False
e) True
f) False

Q3 a) A water vapour / oxygen
B water vapour / oxygen
C carbon dioxide
b) diffusion
c) It's controlled by guard cells, which open and close the stomata to allow or prevent the gases diffusing in and out.
d) 1. The underside of the leaf.
2. The walls of the cells within the leaf.
e) It increases the surface area of the leaf, which increases its effectiveness at gas exchange / means it can collect more light for a given volume.

Q4 gases, dissolved, maximise, thin, short, large, blood, ventilated, bigger, complex, long

Q5 a)

Plant	In a room (% change in mass)	Next to a fan (% change in mass)	By a lamp (% change in mass)	Next to a fan and by a lamp (% change in mass)
1	5	8	10	13
2	5	9	11	15
3	4	11	9	13
Average	4.7	9.3	10	13.7

b) next to a fan and by a lamp
c) To improve the accuracy of her results / make them more reliable.
d) Less water would have been lost since most water loss occurs through stomata that are located mainly on the undersides of leaves.
e)

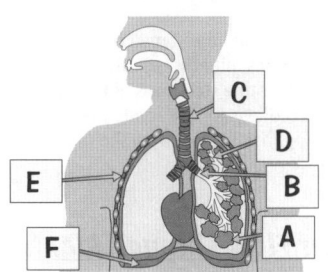

Page 5 — The Breathing System

Q1 a) The movement of air into and out of the lungs.
b) It's needed so that oxygen from the air can diffuse into the bloodstream (and to the cells for respiration) and so that carbon dioxide can diffuse out of the blood.

Q2 a)

b) i) in, intercostal, diaphragm, flattens, up, out, increase, fall, drawn into
ii) relax, ribcage, down, in, volume, decreases, rises, forced out of

Q3 a) A machine that moves air into or out of the lungs.
b) Air is pumped into the lungs, which expands the ribcage. When it stops pumping, the ribcage relaxes and pushes air back out of the lungs.

Page 6 — Diffusion Through Cell Membranes

Q1a) E.g. the alveoli of the lungs, the villi of the small intestine /ileum
b) E.g. oxygen and digested food (glucose)

Biology 3a — Life Processes

Q2 a)

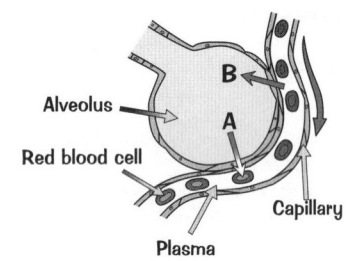

Labels: B, Alveolus, A, Red blood cell, Capillary, Plasma

b) A: oxygen
   B: carbon dioxide
c) diffusion

Q3 a)

Size (cm)	Surface area (cm²)	Time taken for dye uptake (s)
1 x 1 x 1	6	41.6
2 x 2 x 2	24	9.3
5 x 5 x 5	150	1.7
10 x 10 x 10	600	0.4

b) i) bigger
   ii) increases
c) Villi provide a greater surface area in the gut. As this increases the rate of uptake increases, so nutrients are absorbed more quickly.
d) E.g. a good blood supply

Page 7 — Active Transport

Q1 a) False
   b) True
   c) True
Q2 a) root hair cell
   b) Absorbing water and mineral ions from the soil.
   c) The soil generally has a lower concentration of minerals than the root hair cells. Diffusion only takes place from areas of higher concentration to areas of lower concentration.
   d) The concentration of minerals in the soil is lower than in root hair cells. The cells use active transport to absorb the minerals. This requires energy, which is released by respiration.
Q3 a) Any two from, e.g: add the same concentration of potassium ions to the solutions initially / use the same amount of solution / use the same size/mass of barley seedling / examine the seedlings for the same amount of time.
   b) X. The seedling that has taken up the more potassium ions grows better.
   c) 7.5 units

Page 8 — Water Flow Through Plants

Q1 a) b) c) E.g.

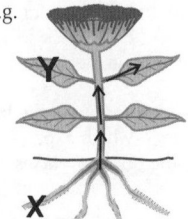

Labels: Y, X

Q2 leaves, evaporation/diffusion, diffusion/evaporation, leaf, xylem, roots, transpiration stream
Q3 a) xylem, phloem
   b) i) xylem
   ii) roots, stem/leaves, leaves/stem
   c) i) phloem
   ii) leaves, growing, storage

Pages 9-10 — Circulatory System — The Heart

Q1 a) False
   b) True
   c) True
   d) False
Q2 a) pulmonary artery
   b) vena cava
   c) right atrium
   d) right ventricle
   e) aorta
   f) pulmonary vein
   g) valves
   h) left ventricle
   i) To prevent the backflow of blood.
   j) double, heart, lungs, oxygenated, deoxygenated
Q3 E.g. function 1: Delivering substances to cells.
   Substances transported: glucose and oxygen.
   E.g. function 2: Removing waste products.
   Substances transported: carbon dioxide and urea.
Q4 atria, ventricles, ventricles, out, organs, arteries, veins
Q5 A: Pulmonary artery
   B: Aorta
   C: Vena cava
   D: Pulmonary vein

Page 11 — Circulatory System — Blood Vessels

Q1 a) The walls are only one cell thick to allow substances to pass through more easily / there is a shorter distance for diffusion.
   b) oxygen, carbon dioxide
   c) E.g. glucose/food
Q2 a) Artery – A , Vein — B
   b) i) Arteries carry blood away from the heart at high pressure so they need to be strong and able to stretch and spring back.
   ii) Veins carry blood back to the heart at low pressure. Valves prevent the blood flowing back in the wrong direction.
Q3 a) E.g. the vein has a wider lumen / thinner wall / valves.
   b) The length of the blood vessel, because this is the dependent variable.
   c) The vein, because it has a thinner wall.
   d) To make his experiment a fair test (the vessels are the same age, etc.)

Page 12 — Circulatory System — The Blood

Q1 a) False
   b) False
   c) False
   d) True
   e) True
   f) False
   g) True
Q2 a) i) haemoglobin
   ii) oxyhaemoglobin
   b) 365 / 120 ≈ 3
Q3 They engulf microorganisms and break them down.
   They produce antibodies that attack microorganisms.
   They produce antitoxins to neutralise the toxins produced by microorganisms.
Q4 a) E.g. red blood cells, white blood cells, platelets, glucose, amino acids, carbon dioxide, urea, hormones, antibodies, antitoxins.
   b)

Substance	Travelling from	Travelling to
Urea	Liver	Kidneys
Carbon dioxide	Organs / cells	Lungs
Glucose	Gut / small intestine	Organs / cells

Biology 3a — Life Processes

Page 13 — Circulation Aids

Q1 tubes, arteries, narrow, open, muscles, beating, heart attack, coronary, irritate, scar tissue, clotting

Q2 a) C
b) D
c) B
d) A

Q3 a) E.g. it won't be rejected by the body's immune system.
b) Any two from, e.g: surgery to fit an artificial heart can lead to bleeding and infection. / Artificial hearts don't work as well as healthy natural ones — parts of the heart could wear out or the electrical motor could fail. / Blood doesn't flow through artificial hearts as smoothly, which can cause blood clots and lead to strokes. / The patient may have to take drugs to thin their blood, which can cause problems with bleeding if they're hurt in an accident.

Page 14 — Homeostasis

Q1 Homeostasis is the maintenance of a constant internal environment.

Q2 a) via the lungs when you breathe out
b) E.g. urea

Q3 a) The thermoregulatory centre in the brain detects the temperature of the blood.
b) from temperature receptors in the skin

Q4 a)

	Too hot	Too cold
hair	hairs lie down flat	hairs stand up
sweat glands	more sweat produced	less sweat produced
blood vessels	dilate near skin	constrict near skin

b) When you shiver, muscles contract automatically. This needs respiration, which releases some energy to warm the body.

Page 15 — The Kidneys and Homeostasis

Q1 a) False
b) True
c) True
d) False
e) True

Q2 a) They're taken into the body in food and drink, and then absorbed into the blood.
b) E.g. too much or too little water would be drawn into the cells, which would damage the cells / so the cells wouldn't work properly.

Q3

	Do you sweat **a lot** or **a little**?	Is the amount of urine you produce **high** or **low**?	Is the urine you produce **more** or **less** concentrated?
Hot Day	A lot	low	more
Cold Day	A little	high	less

Q4 a) i) ions, sugar
ii) Ions — to replace those lost in sweat.
Sugar — to replace the sugar that's used up by muscles during exercise.
b) E.g. whether a scientific study has been carried out that's published in a reputable journal.

Page 16 — Kidney Function

Q1 E, B, D, C, A

Q2 a) i) ions, water, sugar, urea
ii) ions, water, sugar
iii) ions (excess), water (excess), urea
b) Active transport is used to absorb ions and sugar.
Water moves by osmosis (a special type of diffusion).

c) i) protein and red blood cells
ii) They are too big.

Q3 Subject 2 might have kidney damage because they have glucose and a lot of protein in their urine.

Pages 17-18 — Kidney Failure

Q1

Feature of treatment	Dialysis	Transplant
High risk of infection	✓	✓
Long-term, one-off treatment		✓
Patient can lead a relatively normal life		✓
Patient must take drugs		✓
Patient usually needs to live near a hospital	✓	

Q2 a) i) proteins and red blood cells
ii) They are too big to fit through the membrane, so they will remain in the blood.
b) urea
c) It is equal to prevent the diffusion of glucose out of the bloodstream and into the fluid, as it would then be lost from the patient's body.

Q3 a) Because the antigens are foreign / not recognised by the patient's body.
b) E.g. a donor with a tissue type that closely matches the patient is chosen. The patient takes drugs to suppress their immune system.

Q4 a) 1. A needle is inserted into a blood vessel in the patient's arm to remove blood.
2. The patient's blood flows into the dialysis machine and between partially permeable membranes that are surrounded by dialysis fluid.
3. Excess water, ions and wastes are filtered out of the blood and pass into the dialysis fluid.
4. Dialysis continues until nearly all the waste and excess substances are removed.
5. Blood is returned to the patient's body using a vein in their arm.
b) So that useful dissolved ions won't be lost from the blood during dialysis (by diffusion).
c) To keep the concentrations of dissolved substances in the blood at normal levels.

Q5 a) and b)

	Year	
	2004	2013
Total number of patients with kidney failure	37 000	68 000
Number receiving dialysis	20 500	**38 000**
Number that have received a transplant	**16 500**	30 000

c) i) 30 000 − (20 000 + 6500) = £3500
ii) (30 000 × 3) − (20 000 + (6500 × 3)) = £50 500

Pages 19-20 — Controlling Blood Glucose

Q1 a) from digested food and drink
b) E.g. pancreas
c) insulin and glucagon

Q2 Missing words are: insulin, pancreas, insulin, liver, glycogen, glucose, blood, reduced / lower.

Q3 Glucagon is secreted by the pancreas. This makes the liver turn glycogen into glucose. Glucose is added by the liver into the blood. So the blood glucose level increases.

Q4 a) A condition where the pancreas produces little or no insulin so a person's blood sugar level can get too high.
b) E.g. by limiting their intake of foods rich in simple carbohydrates. By taking regular exercise. By undergoing insulin therapy.

Q5 a) i) Diabetics used to use insulin from animals such as pigs. Now they can use human insulin produced by genetically modified bacteria.
ii) It doesn't cause adverse reactions in patients, like animal insulin did.

Biology 3b — Humans and Their Environment

b) i) A pancreas transplant.
ii) E.g. risk of rejecting the organ, having to take immunosuppressive drugs.
c) E.g. artificial pancreases, using stem cells

Page 21 — Mixed Questions — Biology 3a

Q1 a) E.g. a large surface area for diffusion to occur. A moist lining for dissolving gases. Very thin walls so there's a short distance for substance to diffuse across. A good blood supply to get stuff into and out of the blood quickly.
b) i) red blood cells
ii) haemoglobin
iii) They have a large surface area for absorbing oxygen. They have no nucleus to make more room for haemoglobin (which carries oxygen).
Q2 a) root hair cell
b) It gives the cell a large surface area.
c) Minerals are absorbed by active transport, whereas water is not. If respiration stops there will be no energy to power active transport, so no minerals will be absorbed.
d) i) It escapes by diffusion.
ii) hot, dry and windy conditions
iii) oxygen, (allow CO_2 at night)

Biology 3b — Humans and Their Environment

Pages 22-23 — Human Impact on the Environment

Q1 a) bigger
b) faster
c) greater
Q2 a) i) John is more likely to live in the UK and Derek in Kenya.
ii) The following should be ticked:
John buys more belongings, which use more raw materials to manufacture.
John has central heating in his home but Derek has a wood fire.
John drives a car and Derek rides a bicycle.
b) Any sensible suggestion, such as: John could use his car less, use his central heating less, recycle more waste, buy fewer new things, etc.
Q3 a) i) Decrease
ii) E.g. there will be less land for the voles to build their nests on. / The voles will have less of the resources they need, like food and water.
b) Any two from: e.g. building / dumping waste / quarrying
Q4 a)

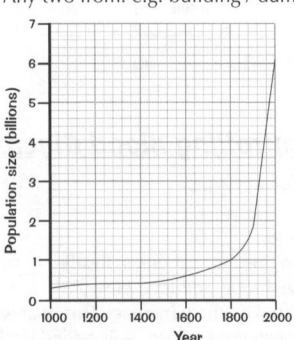

b) Any 2 from: Improvements in medicine meant that fewer people died of diseases. More efficient farming methods produced more food so fewer people died of hunger. Living standards improved over much of the world. Hygiene and sanitation improved over much of the world, etc.
c) It means we are producing more waste.
Q5 a) E.g. pesticides/insecticides, herbicides/weedkillers, fertilisers.
b) E.g. these chemicals can build up on land and might not be easily broken down. The excess may wash into rivers and lakes and pollute the water. These chemicals can harm living things.

Page 24 — Carbon Dioxide and the Greenhouse Effect

Q1 carbon dioxide, burning, global warming, sequestered, oceans, less
Q2 The greenhouse effect is needed for life on Earth as we know it.
Increasing amounts of greenhouse gases cause global warming.
Q3 a) The greenhouses gases absorb much of the heat that is radiated away from Earth and re-radiate it in all directions. This keeps the atmosphere relatively warm.
b) All the energy radiated out by the Earth would be lost. This means that the Earth would be much colder.
c) More greenhouse gas in the atmosphere means that more of the Sun's heat is trapped rather than radiated back out into space. This means the Earth gets warmer.

Page 25 — Deforestation and the Destruction of Peat Bogs

Q1 a) During deforestation, trees are burnt to clear the land, releasing carbon dioxide into the air. Microorganisms feed on bits of dead wood that remain and release carbon dioxide as they respire. Trees take in carbon dioxide for use in photosynthesis, so if there are fewer trees less carbon dioxide is absorbed from the atmosphere.
b) i) false
ii) true
c) E.g. to provide timber for building, to produce paper from wood.
Q2 a) The variety of different species in a habitat.
b) We could miss out on things like new medicines, foods or fibres.
Q3 a) Plants that live in bogs don't fully decay when they die, because there's not enough oxygen. The partly-rotted plants build up to form peat.
b) Carbon is stored in the dead plants that make up the peat. As a bog is drained, the peat starts to decompose and carbon dioxide is released.
c) Use peat-free compost to reduce the demand for peat.

Page 26 — Climate Change

Q1 1. Higher temperatures make ice melt.
2. Sea levels start to rise.
3. Low-lying areas are at risk of flooding.
Q2 a) reduce
b) north
c) cooler, less
d) extreme
Q3 They might be right, but we can't know for sure from such small amounts of evidence. Both students would need to carry out long-term studies using a lot more data.
Q4 a) evidence: data that either supports or contradicts a particular hypothesis.
hypothesis: a possible explanation for a set of observations.
b) E.g. snow and ice cover, the temperature of the sea surface, the speed and the direction of ocean currents, atmospheric temperatures.

Page 27 — Biofuels

Q1 a) respiration
b) anaerobic
c) ethanol
d) Ethanol
Q2 a) E.g. glucose
b) E.g. sugar cane / maize
Q3 generator, batch, waste, carbohydrates, fermented, heating, turbine

Chemistry 3a — Elements, Water and Organic Chemistry

Q4 a) methane and carbon dioxide
b) E.g. any two from: human sewage, animal dung, kitchen waste (e.g. vegetable peelings), agricultural / plant waste (e.g. fallen leaves), sludge waste from factories (e.g. sugar factories)

Pages 28-29 — Using Biogas Generators

Q1 a) Waste material is being fermented / broken down by the anaerobic respiration of microorganisms.
b) The balloon will inflate.
c) The microorganisms will grow faster (and produce more biogas) at a warmer temperature.
Q2 a) About 45 °C.
b) E.g. because heat will be produced during the process.
c) E.g. any two from: amount of waste, amount of bacteria, surface area / size of waste particles, pH, presence of toxins
d) The toxins would poison the microorganisms and inhibit the breakdown of the material.
Q3 a) batch
b) continuous
c) all the time
d) continuous
Q4 a) i) So that the houses are not near the smell.
ii) It will be easier to transport animal dung to the generator.
iii) To keep it warm so the microorganisms can work effectively.
b) E.g. any two from: lower cost fuel, it disposes of their waste, improves the properties of the dung as a fertiliser, less disease and pollution from waste, no need to spend hours collecting wood for fuel.
Q5 a) Energy from the Sun was incorporated into plants by photosynthesis. Some of this energy is then passed to animals when they eat the plants.
b) i) Although it produces carbon dioxide, it is derived from recent photosynthesis, which used up the same amount of carbon dioxide. So, there's no net production of carbon dioxide.
ii) E.g. doesn't produce significant amounts of sulfur dioxide or nitrous oxides which cause acid rain. / Burning methane means it's not released into the atmosphere to contribute to global warming. / Waste is removed which would otherwise cause pollution and disease.

Page 30 — Managing Food Production

Q1 a) Wheat → Human
b) There are fewer steps in this food chain so less energy is lost.
Q2 a) *Fusarium*
b) fermenters, glucose syrup, oxygen, purified
Q3 a) The animals are kept close together, indoors and in small pens, so they're warm and can't move about.
b) The pigs don't waste energy on movement or give out much energy as heat. So the transfer of energy from the feed to the pigs is more efficient — they grow faster on less food.
c) E.g. the pork is cheaper.

Page 31 — Problems With Food Production and Distribution

Q1 a)

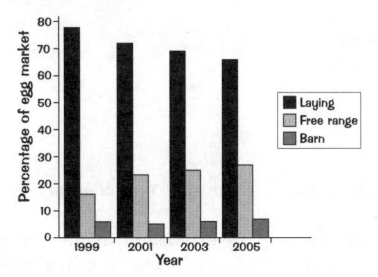

b) Laying –12%
Barn 1%
Free range 11%
c) E.g. more people are choosing not to buy eggs that have been produced by hens kept in distressing conditions / more people choose to buy eggs produced by hens kept in healthy conditions because they're concerned for the hens' wellbeing / more people believe that eggs produced by healthy, free range chickens will taste better
Q2 Products with lots of food miles are transported a long way from where they're produced to where they're sold. This means burning fossil fuels, which releases carbon dioxide into the atmosphere, contributing to global warming.
Q3 a) Fishing quotas put limits on the number and size of fish that can be caught in certain areas. This prevents certain species from being overfished.
b) Having enough food without using resources faster than they renew.

Page 32 — Mixed Questions — Biology 3b

Q1 a) i) crowded, easy
ii) antibiotics
iii) increases
b) biogas
Q2 a) Average surface temperatures have generally been increasing since 1859.
b) i) Methane.
ii) E.g. cow rearing / rice growing / rotting plants.
c) The amounts of carbon dioxide, methane and nitrous oxide have increased since the Industrial Revolution. The global temperature has also increased over the same time. The two may be related, as extra greenhouse gases will absorb more heat, warming the Earth. But there's no definite proof in these two graphs of a direct cause and effect relationship between the two variables.

Chemistry 3a — Elements, Water and Organic Chemistry

Page 33 — History of the Periodic Table

Q1 a) atomic number
b) atomic mass
Q2 a) true
b) false
c) true
d) false
Q3 a) germanium, 5.32 g/cm³
b) i) E.g. they both arranged the elements in order of atomic mass. / They both arranged elements with similar properties into groups.
ii) Unlike Newlands, Mendeleev left gaps for undiscovered elements.
iii) Any one from: e.g. he didn't leave gaps for undiscovered elements. / His groups contained elements with different properties. / His groups mixed up metals and non-metals.
Q4 When elements are arranged in order of atomic mass, a periodic pattern in their properties can be seen.

Pages 34-35 — The Modern Periodic Table

Q1 fun, predicting, properties, discovered, atomic number, chemical
Q2 a) K
b) Li
c) K
Q3 a) The number of outer electrons is the same as the group number.
b) magnesium = 2, 8, 2
oxygen = 2, 6
sulfur = 2, 8, 6

Chemistry 3a — Elements, Water and Organic Chemistry

c) Fluorine is more reactive than chlorine because its outer shell of electrons is closer to the nucleus, so it attracts electrons more strongly.

Q4 a) i) The outer electrons are further from the nucleus and so aren't attracted to the nucleus as strongly.
ii) more reactive
b) i) Fluorine's outermost shell is closer to the nucleus than bromine's so the attraction is greater.
ii) The reactivity decreases down the group because the attraction for electrons decreases.

Q5 a) Group 1
b) These elements would be less reactive. As you go down a group, elements contain more shells of electrons, so there's an increased distance from the nucleus. The outer electron's more easily lost.

Page 36 — Group 1 — The Alkali Metals

Q1 a) false
b) false
c) true
d) true
e) false

Q2 sodium hydroxide, hydrogen, electron, positive

Q3 The metals get more reactive further down the group because the outer electron is more easily lost as it's further from the nucleus.

Q4 a) Lithium is less dense than water.
b) alkaline
c) i) lithium + water → lithium hydroxide + hydrogen
ii) $2Li_{(s)} + 2H_2O_{(l)} \rightarrow 2LiOH_{(aq)} + H_{2(g)}$

Page 37 — Group 7 — The Halogens

Q1 a) false
b) true
c) false
d) true

Q2 The halogens exist as molecules — which are pairs of atoms.
A more reactive halogen — will displace a less reactive one.
The halogens react with metals — to form ionic compounds.
The reactivity of the halogens — decreases as you move down the group.

Q3 a) iron bromide
b) ionic bonding

Q4 a) Bromine is more reactive than iodine so displaces it from the potassium iodide solution. Bromine is less reactive than chlorine so doesn't displace it from potassium chloride solution.
b) $Br_{2(aq)} + 2KI_{(aq)} \rightarrow I_{2(aq)} + 2KBr_{(aq)}$

Pages 38-39 — Transition Elements

Q1

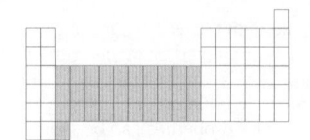

Q2 less, higher, higher, harder, coloured, catalysts

Q3 high density

Q4 a) iron — ammonia production
nickel — converting oils into fats for making margarine
manganese(IV) oxide — decomposition of hydrogen peroxide
b) i) Fe^{2+}, Fe^{3+}
ii) Cu^+, Cu^{2+}
iii) Cr^{2+}, Cr^{3+}

Q5 a) crystals of different colours
b) The crystals won't be colourful. Only transition metals form coloured compounds.

Q6 Found in the block between Groups 2 and 3 of the periodic table.
Has a high melting point.
Has a high density.
Has a shiny appearance.
Forms coloured compounds.
Forms two different chlorides / forms ions with different charges.

Pages 40-41 — Hardness of Water

Q1 a) true
b) false
c) false
d) false
e) true
f) true
g) true
h) false

Q2 a) The kettle becomes less efficient / takes longer to boil.
b) E.g. calcium ions are good for healthy bones and teeth. / It could help reduce the risk of heart disease.

Q3 Permanent — Dissolved calcium sulfate
Temporary — Hydrogencarbonate ions

Q4 a) Ion exchange columns have lots of sodium or hydrogen ions which they exchange for calcium and magnesium ions, removing them from the water.
b) This works for both types of hardness.

Q5 a) calcium carbonate
b) i) A and B
ii) B
iii) A
iv) C
c) i) Permanent hardness is not removed by boiling.
ii) sodium carbonate (Na_2CO_3)/washing soda
d) i) Source A
ii) The reduction in the amount of soap needed to create a lather in water from this source after it had been boiled was the greatest.

Page 42 — Water Quality

Q1 a) distilled water
b) It is made by boiling water and condensing the steam which takes a lot of energy / is a very expensive process.

Q2 A — The water passes through a mesh screen to remove bits like twigs.
B — Chemicals are added to make solids and microbes stick together and fall to the bottom.
C — The water is filtered to remove all solids.
D — Chlorine is added to kill any remaining harmful microbes.

Q3 a) tooth decay, disease, cancer, bone, toxic
b) They could buy a water filter containing carbon.

Pages 43-44 — Reversible Reactions

Q1 products, react, reactants, balance, closed, escape

Q2 a) i) A, B
ii) AB
b) i) Y
ii) X
c) $A + B \rightleftharpoons AB$
d) at the same rate

Q3 a) True
b) False
c) True
d) False

Q4 a) It takes in heat because it must be endothermic.
b) backward
c) All reversible reactions are exothermic in one direction and endothermic in the other, so temperature will always change the position of equilibrium.
d) It will have no effect because both sides of the reaction have the same number of molecules/volume.

Chemistry 3b — Titrations, Energy and Chemical Tests

Q5 a) i) Forward, because there are three molecules on the left-hand side of the reaction and only two molecules on the right-hand side of the reaction.

ii) It moves it to the right / increases the amount of SO_3 produced.

b) B

c) It stays the same.

Page 45 — The Haber Process

Q1 a) $N_{2(g)} + 3H_{2(g)} \rightleftharpoons 2NH_{3(g)}$

b) E.g. air (nitrogen) and natural gas (hydrogen).

Q2 a) 200 atmospheres, 450 °C.

b) 1. High enough to give a good % yield.
2. Not so high that the plant becomes too expensive to build.

Q3 a) It will reduce the amount of ammonia formed.

b) To increase the rate of reaction.

c) They are recycled.

Q4 a) It has no effect on % yield.

b) It makes it cheaper to produce. The rate of reaction is increased without an expensive increase in temperature or pressure.

Pages 46-47 — Alcohols

Q1

Alcohol	No. of Carbon Atoms	Molecular Formula	Displayed Formula
Methanol	1	CH_3OH	H–C–O–H
Ethanol	2	C_2H_5OH	H–C–C–O–H
Propanol	3	C_3H_7OH	H–C–C–C–O–H

Q2 a) the $-OH$ group

b) This shows the molecule's functional $-OH$ group (and tells you more about the structure).

Q3 a) $C_2H_5OH_{(l)} + 3O_{2(g)} \rightarrow 2CO_{2(g)} + 3H_2O_{(g)}$

b) petrol, fuel, less, fermentation, renewable, land/sunshine, sunshine/land

Q4 a) False

b) False

c) True

d) False

e) True

f) True

g) True

Q5 dissolve, oils/fats, fats/oils, solvents, perfumes, oils, water

Q6 a) To stop people drinking it by mistake as it is toxic.

b) E.g. cleaning paint brushes and as a fuel

Page 48 — Carboxylic Acids

Q1 a) True

b) False

c) False

Q2

Carboxylic acid	No. of Carbon Atoms	Molecular Formula	Displayed Formula
Methanoic Acid	1	HCOOH	
Ethanoic Acid	2	CH_3COOH	
Propanoic Acid	3	C_2H_5COOH	

Q3 a) i) microbes

ii) oxidising agents

b) i) Carboxylic acids don't ionise completely so not many H^+ ions (responsible for making a solution acidic) are released.

ii) vinegar

c) lower

Page 49 — Esters

Q1 a) esters

b) don't, do

c) are

d) flammable, fire

e) -COO-

Q2

and methyl ethanoate

Q3 a) concentrated sulfuric acid

b) ethanol + **ethanoic acid** → ethyl ethanoate + **water**

Q4 a) Some esters are toxic, especially in large doses. / Some people worry about health problems with synthetic food additives.

b) E.g. perfumes

Pages 50-51 — Mixed Questions — Chemistry 3a

Q1 Any two from: e.g. they have pleasant smells. / They are volatile. / They mix well with other solvents.

Q2 a) Atomic mass

b) He left gaps for undiscovered elements.

c) 1

d) Group 2

Q3 a) $Cl_{2(aq)} + 2KBr_{(aq)} \rightarrow Br_{2(aq)} + 2KCl_{(aq)}$

b) Bromine is less reactive than chlorine, so it doesn't displace it from the solution.

Q4 a) $N_2 + 3H_2 \rightleftharpoons 2NH_3$

b) i) increase

ii) If you raise the pressure it encourages the reaction that produces less volume (molecules). The forward reaction produces less volume (molecules).

c) decrease

Q5 a) F.
Any two from: it has a high melting point. / It has a high density. / It is a good conductor of electricity.

b) It is used as a catalyst (transition metals make good catalysts).

Q6 a) i) Any one from: B, C or D

ii) E

iii) D

b) ionic, water, hydrogen, hydroxide

Q7 a) B

b) A

c) Boiling removes temporary hardness from water. River A must contain both permanent and temporary hardness. Once the temporary hardness was removed, less soap was needed to form a lasting lather.

Chemistry 3b — Titrations, Energy and Chemical Tests

Page 52 — Titration

Q1 a) i) Universal indicator changes colour gradually — titrations need a definite colour change.

ii) Any one from: e.g. phenolphthalein / methyl orange

b) Put some of the sodium hydroxide in a flask, along with some indicator.
Add the sulfuric acid, a bit at a time, to the sodium hydroxide using a burette — giving the flask a regular swirl.
Go especially slowly (a drop at a time) when you think the sodium hydroxide's almost neutralised.
The indicator will change colour when it is.
Record the amount of sulfuric acid used to neutralise the sodium hydroxide.
Repeat this process a few times and take the mean of your results.

Chemistry 3b — Titrations, Energy and Chemical Tests

c)

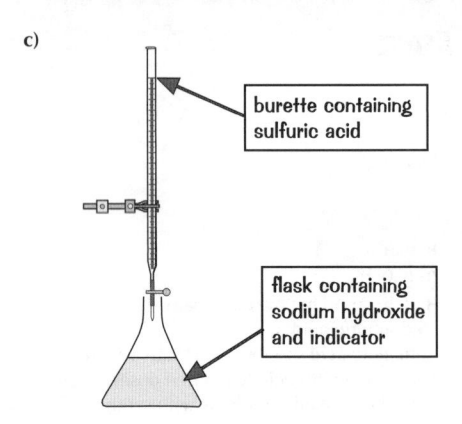

burette containing
sulfuric acid

flask containing
sodium hydroxide
and indicator

Pages 53-54 — Titration Calculations

Q1 a) $2 \times 1 = 2$ moles
b) $1 \times (100 \div 1000) = 0.1$ moles
c) $0.1 \times (25 \div 1000) = 0.0025$ moles
d) $0.2 \times (10 \div 1000) = 0.002$ moles
Q2 a) $HCl + NaOH \rightarrow \textbf{NaCl} + \textbf{H}_2\textbf{O}$
b) $H_2SO_4 + \textbf{2} KOH \rightarrow \textbf{K}_2\textbf{SO}_4 + \textbf{2H}_2\textbf{O}$
Q3 a) i) $0.5 \times (23 + 16 + 1) = 20$ g
ii) $0.2 \times (2 + 32 + 64) = 19.6$ g
iii) $0.02 \times (40 + 32 + 2) = 1.48$ g
b) i) $0.1 \times (39 + 16 + 1) = 5.6$ g/dm³
ii) $2 \times (1 + 14 + 48) = 126$ g/dm³
Q4 a) $0.1 \times (20 \div 1000) = 0.002$ moles
b) $\textbf{HCl} + \textbf{NaOH} \rightarrow \textbf{NaCl} + \textbf{H}_2\textbf{O}$
c) From the equation, **1** mole of HCl reacts with **1** mole of NaOH
d) $0.002 \div 1 = 0.002$ moles
e) $0.002 \div (25 \div 1000) = 0.08$ mol/dm³
f) Concentration $= 0.08 \times (23 + 16 + 1) = 3.2$ g/dm³
Q5 a) i) Moles KOH $= 0.1 \times (30 \div 1000) = 0.003$
ii) Reaction equation: $2KOH + H_2SO_4 \rightarrow K_2SO_4 + 2H_2O$, so $0.003 \div 2 = 0.0015$ moles of H_2SO_4.
iii) Concentration of $H_2SO_4 = 0.0015 \div (10 \div 1000)$ $= 0.15$ mol/dm³
b) Mass in grams $= 0.15 \times (2 + 32 + 64) = 14.7$ g/dm³

Page 55 — Energy

Q1 energy, exothermic, heat, an increase, endothermic, heat, a decrease
Q2 a) $29.5\ °C - 22\ °C = \textbf{7.5 °C}$ (accept between 7 and 8 °C)
b) neutralisation, exothermic
c) Some energy is always lost to the surroundings.
Q3 a) break
b) formed
c) endothermic
d) exothermic
Q4 a) exothermic
b) A–C, because more energy is released when this bond forms than is used breaking the bond in A–B.

Page 56 — Energy and Fuels

Q1 a) Because copper is such a good conductor of heat.
b) Because heat energy is lost, e.g. in heating the can and the surrounding air.
Q2 a) Energy transferred $= 50 \times 4.2 \times 30.5 = 6405$ J
b) Energy per gram $= 6405 \div 0.7 = 9150$ J/g $= 9.15$ kJ/g
Q3 a) Energy transferred $= 50 \times 4.2 \times 27 = 5670$ J
Energy released per gram $= 5670 \div 0.8 = 7087.5$ J/g $= 7.09$ kJ/g
b) Petrol, because it releases more energy per gram of fuel than fuel X does.
Q4 a) E.g. carbon dioxide/CO_2
b) Any one from: e.g. global warming / climate change

c) As it is running out it will get more expensive. This means that everything that's transported by lorry, train or plane will get more expensive too.

Pages 57-58 — Bond Energies

Q1 a) A, C and D
b) B
c) B and E
d) C
Q2 a) endothermic
b) The minimum energy needed by reacting particles to break their bonds.
c) They speed up chemical reactions by providing a different pathway with a lower activation energy (so the reaction happens more easily and more quickly).
Q3 a) Energy change $= -90$ kJ/mol.
b) Activation energy $= +70$ kJ/mol.
c)

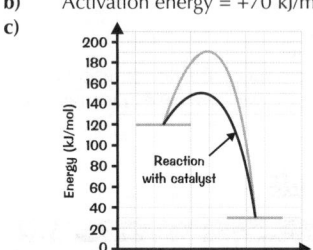

Q4 a) $(4 \times 412) + (2 \times 498) = 2644$ kJ/mol.
b) $(2 \times 743) + (4 \times 463) = 3338$ kJ/mol.
c) Energy change $= 2644 - 3338 = -694$ kJ/mol.
Q5 Energy needed to break bonds $=$ $[158 + (4 \times 391) + 498] = 2220$. Energy released when bonds made $=$ $[945 + (4 \times 463)] = 2797$. So overall energy change $= 2220 - 2797 = -577$ kJ/mol.
Q6 Energy needed to break bonds $=$ $[(2 \times 348) + (12 \times 412) + (7 \times 498)] = 9126$. Energy released when bonds made $=$ $[(8 \times 743) + (12 \times 463)] = 11\,500$. So overall energy change $= -2374$ kJ/mol.

Page 59 — Getting Energy from Hydrogen

Q1 a) water
b) i) It is very clean as water isn't a pollutant.
ii) Any one from: e.g. you need a special, expensive engine. / You need energy from another source to make hydrogen. / Hydrogen's hard to store safely — it's very explosive.
Q2 fuel, oxygen, electricity
Q3 Fuel cell vehicles don't produce any pollutants — no greenhouse gases, no nitrogen oxides, no sulfur dioxide, no carbon monoxide. The only by-products are water and heat.
Q4 E.g. hydrogen is a gas so it takes up loads more space to store than liquid fuels like petrol. / It's very explosive so it's difficult to store safely. / The hydrogen fuel is often made either from hydrocarbons (from fossil fuels), or by electrolysis of water, which uses electricity (and that electricity's got to be generated somehow — usually this involves fossil fuels).

Pages 60-61 — Tests for Positive Ions

Q1 a) Metals **always** form positive ions.
b) Clean a wire loop by dipping it into hydrochloric acid and rinsing with distilled water. Then dip it in the sample, put it into the clear blue part of a Bunsen flame and observe any colours produced.
c) There could be other substances on the wire that might produce a different flame colour to the test substance.

Physics 3a — Medical Applications of Physics

Q2 a) red flame — Ca^{2+}
yellow flame — Na^+
crimson flame — Li^+
green flame — Ba^{2+}
lilac flame — K^+

b) potassium nitrate

Q3 a)

Positive Ion	Colour of Precipitate
Fe^{2+}	**green**
Cu^{2+}	blue
Fe^{3+}	**brown**
Al^{3+}	**white**

b) $Fe^{2+}_{(aq)} + 2OH^-_{(aq)} \rightarrow$ **$Fe(OH)_{2(s)}$**

c) $Fe^{3+}_{(aq)} + 3OH^-_{(aq)} \rightarrow Fe(OH)_{3(s)}$

d) A white precipitate forms that then dissolves in excess NaOH to form a colourless solution.

Q4 a) $CuSO_4$

b) LiCl

c) $Al_2(SO_4)_3$

d) $FeSO_4$

e) $FeCl_3$

f) $CaCl_2$

Page 62 — Tests for Negative Ions

Q1 a) SO_4^{2-}

b) I^-

c) CO_3^{2-}

Q2 acid, carbon dioxide, limewater

Q3 a) dilute hydrochloric acid, barium chloride solution

b) a white precipitate (of barium sulfate)

Q4 She could add dilute nitric acid to a solution of the compound, and then add some silver nitrate solution. If the compound contains Cl^- ions a white precipitate will form. If it contains Br^- ions a cream precipitate will form and if it contains I^- ions a yellow precipitate will form.

Q5 a) $Ag^+_{(aq)} + Cl^-_{(aq)} \rightarrow AgCl_{(s)}$

b) $2HCl_{(aq)} + Na_2CO_{3(s)} \rightarrow 2NaCl_{(aq)} + H_2O_{(l)} + CO_{2(g)}$

c) $Ba^{2+}_{(aq)} + SO_4^{2-}_{(aq)} \rightarrow BaSO_{4(s)}$

Pages 63-64 — Mixed Questions — Chemistry 3b

Q1 a) An exothermic reaction. It gives out energy to the surroundings.

b) less than

c) E.g. burn the food or fuel and use the energy from the flame to heat up some water. Use the change in water temperature to find the amount of energy.

d) Energy transferred = $100 \times 4.2 \times 15 = 6300$ J
Energy produced per gram = $6300 \div 0.5 = 12\ 600$ J/g
= 12.6 kJ/g

Q2 a) He would see a green precipitate.

b) That the compound contains copper(II)/Cu^{2+} ions.

c) $Cu^{2+}(aq) + 2OH^-(aq) \rightarrow Cu(OH)_{2(s)}$

d) He could add dilute hydrochloric acid/HCl to the compound, followed by barium chloride/$BaCl_2$ and look for a white precipitate.

e) $CuSO_4$

Q3 a) and b)

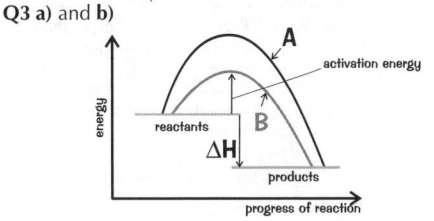

c) B

d) exothermic

Q4 a) Ca^{2+}

b) CO_3^{2-}

c) Fe^{3+}

d) SO_4^{2-}

Q5 a) Any one from: e.g. methyl orange / phenolphthalein

b) i) Moles NaOH = $0.5 \times (20 \div 1000) = 0.01$ moles
NaOH + HCl $\rightarrow$ NaCl + H_2O, so there's also 0.01 moles of HCl.
Concentration of HCl = $0.01 \div (25 \div 1000) = 0.4$ mol/dm³

ii) M_r HCl = 1 + 35.5. = 36.5
In 1 dm³: mass in grams = moles $\times M_r$ = 0.4×36.5
= 14.6 g/dm³

Physics 3a — Medical Applications of Physics

Pages 65-66 — X-rays in Medicine

Q1 a) short, ionisation

b) transmitted, absorbed

c) charge-coupled device

d) atom

Q2 kill, cells, cancer, focused, normal, ill, rotating, centre

Q3 a) E.g. X-rays interact with photographic film in the same way as visible light. The X-ray image is formed by the varying intensities of X-ray beam that are transmitted (i.e. through soft tissue) through to the film. Where the X-rays are transmitted, more X-rays reach the photographic plate causing it to turn dark. This leaves a white image of the denser areas.

b) E.g. A charge-coupled device can be used to form a high resolution image. A CCD is a grid of millions of pixels, each of which is sensitive to X-rays. Each pixel generates an electric signal when it interacts with an X-ray.

c) E.g. bone fractures.

Q4 a) True

b) False

c) False

d) True

Q5 1. The patient is put inside the CT scanner.
2. An X-ray tube emits an X-ray beam whilst rotating around the patient.
3. Detectors on the opposite side of the scanner measure the intensity of the transmitted X-rays.
4. A computer uses the detected X-rays to generate an image of a two-dimensional slice through the body.
5. Multiple slice images are put together to give a three-dimensional picture.

Q6 a) E.g. any two from: wear a lead apron / stand behind a lead screen / leave the room.

b) E.g. any two from: minimise exposure time / avoid repeat X-rays / use lead to shield other areas of the body not being imaged.

Page 67 — Ultrasound

Q1 a) Ultrasound is sound with a frequency above 20 000 Hz — higher than the upper limit of hearing for humans.

b) Electrical devices can be set to produce electrical oscillations at the required frequency. These can be converted into mechanical vibrations (i.e. sound waves).

Q2 E.g.

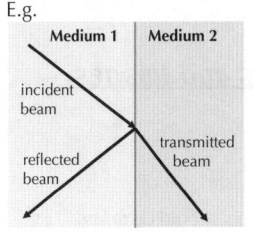

Physics 3a — Medical Applications of Physics

Q3 a) Looking at the oscilloscope trace, there is a 5 μs gap between the start of the trace and the first ultrasound pulse.
s = v × t
v = 1450 m/s, t = 0.000005 s
s = 1450 × 0.000005 = 0.00725
You need to divide by 2 to find the distance between the ultrasound device and the fat boundary:
0.00725 ÷ 2 = **0.003625 m** (= 0.36 cm).

b) The time between traces = 5 × 5 μs = 0.000025 s
Distance = speed × time = 1450 × 0.000025 = 0.03625 m
But this is the distance to travel through the layer of fat and back again so divide by 2 to find the thickness of the layer of fat: 0.03625 ÷ 2 = 0.018125 m = **1.8 cm** (to 1 d.p.)

Page 68 — Ultrasound Uses

Q1 a) It breaks the kidney stones into small particles.
b) They pass out of the body in urine.
c) E.g. it's relatively painless, no surgery is required.
Q2 a)

	Advantage	Disadvantage
Ultrasound imaging	E.g. non-ionising, can image soft tissue	E.g. produces low resolution, fuzzy images
X-ray photographs	E.g. low radiation dose, can image hard tissue, e.g. bone, better resolution than ultrasound images	E.g. the radiation is ionising, images are limited to 2D
CT scans	E.g. produces high resolution images of both hard and soft tissue, can be used to make 3D images	E.g. high radiation dose, expensive

b) E.g. CT scanning, because a high resolution image of both the brain and the skull can be produced.
Q3 a) Ultrasound causes no known damage to cells, whereas X-rays are ionising radiation which can cause cancer.
b) X-rays — they penetrate most of the soft tissues but are absorbed (mostly) by bone. Ultrasound would not give a good picture of the bone as it would be reflected at the boundaries between different layers of soft tissue.

Page 69 — Refractive Index

Q1 a) refraction
b) E.g.

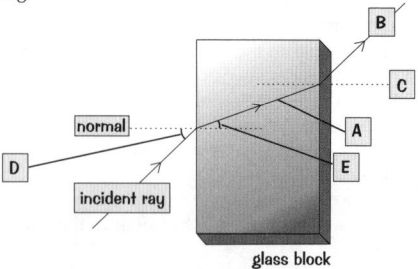

Q2 a) The ratio of the speed of light in a vacuum to the speed of light in that medium.
b) n = sin i / sin r
n = refractive index, i = angle of incidence, r = angle of refraction.
Q3 n = sin 30 ÷ sin 22 = **1.3**.
Q4 n = sin i / sin r, so 1.514 = sin 45 ÷ sin r.
Therefore sin r = sin 45 ÷ 1.514 = 0.467.
Hence r = sin^{-1} (0.467) = **27.8°**.

Pages 70-71 — Lenses and Images

Q1 a) W = incident
X = converging
Y = parallel
Z = focal point
b) The following statements should be ticked:
Any ray passing along the axis
Any ray passing through the centre of the lens

Q2 a) False
b) True
c) True
d) False
Q3 a) D — Either a converging or a diverging lens
b)

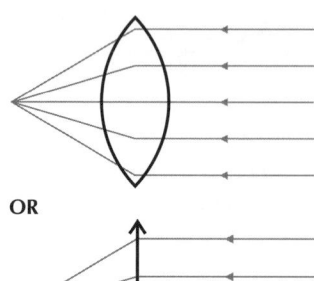

OR

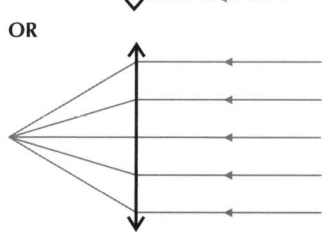

Q4 a) In a real image, the rays from the object actually pass through the image (so it can be projected onto a screen). In a virtual image, the rays only appear to have come from the location of the image.
b) 1. say its size
2. say whether it is upright or inverted
3. say whether it is real or virtual.
Q5 a) The focal point on the other side of the lens.
b) Through the centre of the lens.
c) The top of the image will be where those two rays meet.
Q6

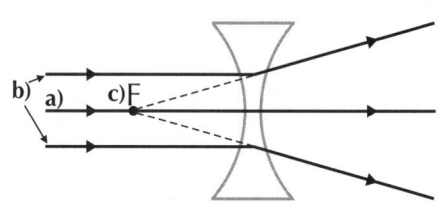

Pages 72-73 — Lenses

Q1

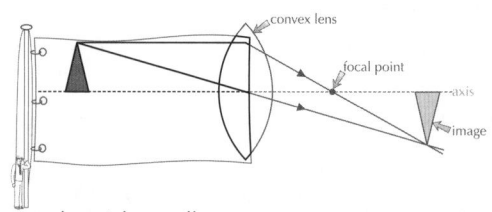

Q2 virtual, upright, smaller.
Q3 a)

Distance from lens to object	Distance from lens to image	Type of image	Size of image
Greater than 2F	Between 2F and F	Real, inverted	Smaller than object
Equal to 2F	**Equal to 2F**	Real, inverted	**Equal to object**
Between 2F and F	Greater than 2F	**Real, inverted**	**Larger than object**
Less than F	Greater than 2F	**Virtual, upright**	Larger than object

b) i) The image will be 1 cm high.
ii) The image will be 5 cm away from the lens on the opposite side from the object.

Physics 3a — Medical Applications of Physics

Q4 a) i) upright
ii) on the same side
iii) virtual
b) C – 10.2 cm

Q5

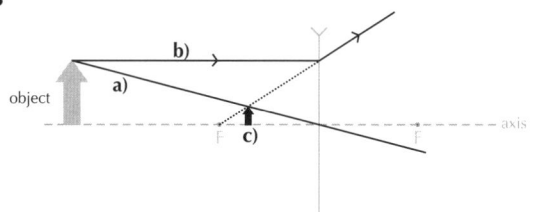

Q6

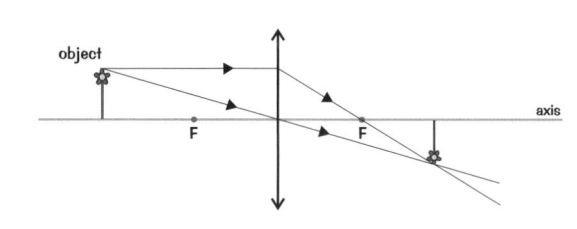

Pages 74-75 — Magnification and Power

Q1 a) A convex / converging lens
b) It is only at a distance nearer than the focal point that you will get an upright, magnified, virtual image.
c) B, D and E should be circled.
Q2 a) Magnification = image height ÷ object height
b) M = 0.8 ÷ 0.5 = 1.6
c) 3 × 1.6 = 4.8 mm
Q3 a) fatter lenses
b) power = 1 ÷ focal length
Q4 a) power = 1 ÷ focal length = 1 ÷ 0.15 = **6.67 D** (to 2 d.p.)
b) focal length = 1 ÷ power = 1 ÷ 5.2 = **0.19 m** (to 2 d.p.)
c) The **power** of a converging lens is **positive**, whereas the **power** of a diverging lens is **negative**.
Q5 a) 1. The curvature of the lens surfaces.
2. The refractive index of the lens material.
b) A material with a higher refractive index was used. For a given focal length, the greater the refractive index the flatter the lens. This means the lens can be manufactured to be thinner.

Pages 76-77 — The Eye

Q1

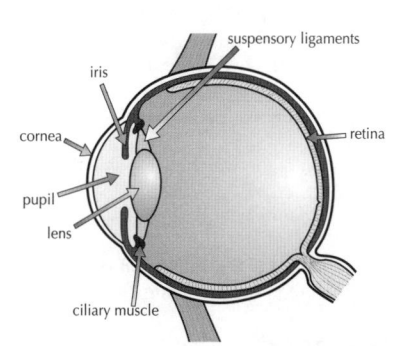

Q2 a) Both are real, inverted images projected onto a "screen" (the film in the case of the camera, the retina in the case of the eye).
b) Because for an object nearer to a converging lens than the focal length, the image formed is virtual. A virtual image can't be projected onto the film.
c) on the film, smaller, retina

Q3

Part of the eye	Function
Lens	Focuses light on the retina
Retina	Light sensitive layer
Ciliary muscles	Cause the lens to change shape
Pupil	Hole through which light enters the eye

Q4 relax, thin, cornea, retina, retina
Q5 a) The near point is **the closest distance that the eye can focus on.**
For normally-sighted adults, the near point is about **25 cm.**
b) The far point is **the furthest distance that the eye can focus on comfortably.**
For normally-sighted adults, the far point is at **infinity**.

Page 78 — Correcting Vision

Q1 a) short, far, far away, in front of
b) 1. Cornea and lens system is too powerful.
2. Eyeball is too long.
c) i) A
ii) A diverging lens of negative power compensates for an overly powerful lens and cornea system. The light from the object is diverged before it enters the eye so that the image is brought into focus at the retina. It makes objects an infinite distance away appear as though they are at the eye's natural far point.
Q2 a) A narrow intense beam of light.
b) i) To burn and seal shut tissue, e.g. blood vessels.
ii) E.g. a surgeon uses a laser to vaporise some of the cornea to change its shape. This can increase or decrease the power of the cornea, and so correct long or short sight.

Page 79 — Total Internal Reflection

Q1 a) Visible light.
b) Glass or perspex/plastic.
c) One bundle brings the light to the area/object in the body that needs to be looked at. The second bundle brings the light from the area/object back to form an image so the area can be viewed.
d) In the left-hand diagram, the angle of incidence is 46° (greater than the critical angle of 42°), so the ray is totally internally reflected. In the second diagram, the angle of incidence is 30°, so the ray is partially reflected, but most of the light passes out of the glass.

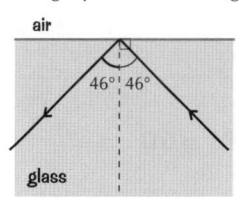 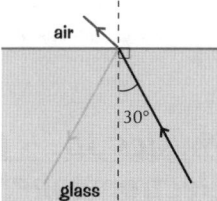

Q2 a) n = 1 ÷ sin c, c = 42°
n = 1 ÷ sin 42 = **1.49**
b) c = sin⁻¹ (1 ÷ n), n = 2.4
c = sin⁻¹ (1 ÷ 2.4) = **24.6°**
c) The diamond ring will be the most sparkly because it has the smaller critical angle, and so will totally internally reflect light from more angles than glass.

Pages 80-82 — Mixed Questions — Physics 3a

Q1 a) i) Medium 1 is glass
Medium 2 is air
ii) The light ray bends away from the normal as it enters medium 2, which shows its speed has increased. Light will speed up as it enters a less dense medium, which means medium 2 must be air.

Physics 3b — Forces and Electromagnetism

b) i) B

ii) Total internal reflection occurs when light is travelling from a dense medium to a less dense medium. B is true because the light is travelling from glass to air — air is less dense than glass.

c) i) n = 1 ÷ sin c, c = 49°, n = 1 ÷ sin 49 = **1.33**

ii) n = sin i ÷ sin r, rearranging gives:
sin r = sin i ÷ n, r = sin⁻¹ (sin i ÷ n)
n = 1.33, i = 20°
r = sin⁻¹ (sin 20 ÷ 1.33) = **14.9°** (to 1 d.p.)

Q2 a)

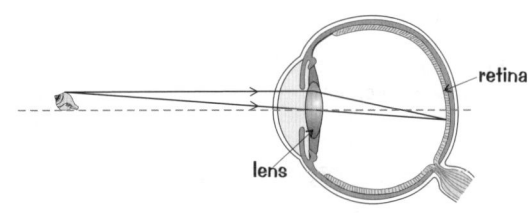

retina

lens

b) short, behind, convex

c) i) Power = 1 ÷ focal length = 1 ÷ 0.4 = **2.5 D**

ii) The left lens is more powerful so will have a more strongly curved surface (the more curved the lens the greater its power).

d) i) 3 cm

ii) 4 ÷ 1.8 = 2.2

iii) Virtual — the light rays don't actually come from where they appear to, and the image can't be projected on a screen.

Q3 a) v = 1500 m/s
d = v × t = 1500 × 0.0000260 = 0.039 m
0.039 ÷ 2 = 0.0195 m ≈ **2 cm**.

b) E.g. X-rays are ionising and are therefore dangerous to the developing fetus. Ultrasound is non-ionising and, as far as anyone can tell, safe. (Ultrasound can image soft tissue whereas X-rays are more suited to imaging dense or hard tissue such as bone.)

c) E.g. X-rays are used to treat cancer because they are ionising. Large doses of ionising radiation can be used to kill cancerous cells. Ultrasound is non-ionising and won't damage cancerous cells.

d) E.g. CT scans use large doses of ionising X-rays which can be damaging to the health of the patient.

e) E.g. an **X-ray tube** fires intense beams of X-rays through the patient. These X-rays are picked up by **detectors** on the opposite side. The X-ray tube and detectors are **rotated** during the scan. A **computer** interprets the different intensities of X-ray signals to form an image of a two-dimensional **slice** of the patient. Multiple two-dimensional CT scans are compiled by the computer to form a three-dimensional image.

Physics 3b — Forces and Electromagnetism

Pages 83-84 — Turning Forces and the Centre of Mass

Q1 a) force, moment, perpendicular, pivot.

b) Nm (newton-metres)

Q2 a) M = F × d = 45 × 0.1 = 4.5 Nm

b) i) B

ii) C

Q3 a)

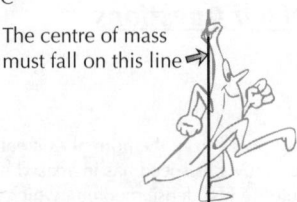

The centre of mass must fall on this line

b) centre of mass, vertically below, perpendicular, moment.

Q4 a)

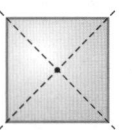 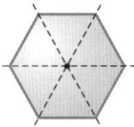

The lines should pass through the middle of each side

b) D

Q5 The weight of the pole acts at its centre of mass. The centre of mass of the pole is 0.4 m from each end. So the weight of 130 N acts 0.4 m from the pivot.
M = F × d = 130 × 0.4 = 52 Nm

Q6 a) Hang the plumb line from the same point as the piece of card. Draw a pencil line on the card along the plumb line. Hang the card in a different position and do the same thing again. Where the two lines cross is the centre of mass.

b) Preferred answer: Repeat the same steps for several pivot points to get multiple lines that will all cross at the centre of mass.
Other acceptable answers: make sure the card is not swaying when the lines are marked / is not moved by marking the lines / is not bent out of shape; make sure the line isn't too thick and is accurately placed.

Page 85 — Balanced Moments and Levers

Q1 a) M = F × d = 2 × 0.2 = 0.4 Nm anticlockwise.

b) M = F × d = 5 × 0.16 = 0.8 Nm anticlockwise.

c) Total anticlockwise moments = total clockwise moments.
0.4 Nm + 0.8 Nm = 8 N × distance
1.2 Nm = 8 N × distance
1.2 ÷ 8 = distance
distance = 0.15 m = 15 cm.

d) No. Since <u>all</u> the moments would be multiplied by 2, it would stay balanced.

Q2 E.g. The wheelbarrow reduces the amount of force needed to give a particular moment. It does this by having long handles which mean that less force is needed to lift the wheelbarrow, as the point at which the force is applied is further away from the pivot (M = F × d).

Q3 The weight acts at the centre of mass = 40 cm from the pivot. The leg is 80 − 5 = 75 cm from the pivot.
Anticlockwise moments = Clockwise moments
40 N × 0.4 m = F × 0.75 m
16 Nm = F × 0.75 m
16 ÷ 0.75 = F
F = 21.3 N

Page 86 — Moments, Stability and Pendulums

Q1 A lot of the mass of the filing cabinet is concentrated in the top draw. So, when the drawer is fully pulled out, the centre of mass could move beyond the edge of the base, making the cabinet unstable.

Q2 C. Because it has the widest base and lowest centre of mass.

Q3 a) The line of action of the weight lies inside the base of the cart.

b) E.g. Having a wider/heavier base to lower the centre of mass.

Q4 a) f = 1 ÷ T, so T = 1 ÷ f = 1 ÷ 1.25 = **0.8 Hz**

b) Increase the length of the pendulum.

Page 87 — Hydraulics

Q1 flow, incompressible, force, transmitted, pressure, equally

Q2 a) They use different cross-sectional areas for the effort and load. P = F ÷ A, so a pressure is created at the first piston using a small force over a small area. Pressure is transmitted equally through a liquid, so the pressure at the second piston is the same. The second piston has a larger area — so there will be a much larger force acting on it.

Physics 3b — Forces and Electromagnetism

b) i)   P = F ÷ A = 650 ÷ 0.0025 = **260 000 Pa** (or N/m²)
ii)   The pressure will be the same (260 000 Pa) because pressure is transmitted equally through a liquid — so the pressure at both pistons will be the same.

Q3 a)   P = F ÷ A = 18 ÷ 0.00012 = **150 000 Pa** (or N/m²)
b)   Pressure at smaller piston = pressure at larger piston, so F = P × A = 150 000 × 0.0003 = **45 N**

Page 88 — Circular Motion

Q1   D — a change in velocity

Q2 a) and b)

Q3 a)   Yes. It is continually changing direction, so it must be changing velocity — accelerating.
b)   The following statements should be ticked:
"If a body is accelerating then there must be a resultant force acting on it."
"If there is no resultant force acting on a body then it carries on moving in a straight line at the same speed."
c)   Centripetal force
d)   A runner running round a circular track — Friction
A satellite in orbit round the Earth — Gravity
The seats at the ends of the spokes of a spinning fairground ride — Tension

Q4 a)   greater
b)   greater
c)   1617 N

Pages 89-90 — Magnetic Fields

Q1   Magnetic fields can exert a force on a wire carrying a current.

Q2

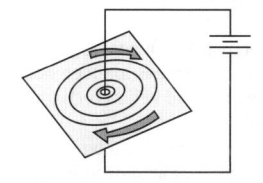

Q3 a)

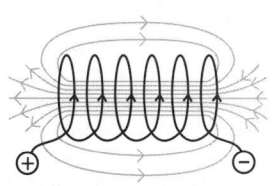

b)   It would exert a force of attraction on it.
c)   electromagnet

Q4   E.g. Unlike ordinary magnets, electromagnets are magnets which can be switched on and off. So they're useful for attracting and picking up magnetic materials (e.g. iron) so they can be moved, but they can then be made to drop the materials by switching off the current.

Q5 a)   When the switch is closed the right-hand contact is attracted towards the solenoid. This breaks the external circuit, turning it off. When the switch is turned off, the solenoid loses its magnetism and the contact is returned to its original position by the spring. This turns the external circuit on again.
b)   The soft iron core makes the solenoid more powerful / It has a stronger magnetic force. Soft iron will lose its magnetism quickly when the electric current is switched off.

Page 91 — The Motor Effect

Q1   magnetic field, permanent magnets, force, current, stronger, angle, motor
Q2 a)   The wire will move out of the paper (towards the reader).
b)   By reversing the direction of the current OR by turning the magnets the other way round (reversing the magnetic field).
Q3   A current-carrying wire will not experience a force if it is parallel to the magnetic field of a permanent magnet.
Q4   The wire will move downwards, at right angles to the magnetic field.

Page 92 — The Simple Electric Motor

Q1   Using a commutator.
Q2   The split-ring commutator reverses the direction of the current every half turn by swapping the contacts to the DC supply.
Q3   By reversing the polarity of the magnets OR by reversing the direction of the current.
Q4   E.g. the axle of the electric motor could be used to turn a (large) pulley wheel, around which the lift cables could wind or unwind to raise or lower the lift.
Q5   current, magnetic, field, force, amplifier, move, frequency, sound.

Page 93 — Electromagnetic Induction

Q1 a)   E.g. Electromagnetic induction is the creation of a potential difference across the ends of a conductor which is experiencing a change in magnetic field (as it 'cuts' through magnetic field lines).
b)   Move the (vertical) wire in and out of the magnetic field at an angle to the direction of the field (i.e. not parallel to the magnetic field).
c)   The ammeter needle would move first in one direction, then back to zero and then in the opposite direction and back to zero again. It would continue like this as long as the wire was moving in and out of the magnetic field.
d)   The ammeter needle would still move from one side to the other, but would start from the opposite side.
Q2 a)   By pulling the magnet out again OR by turning the magnet round and pushing it into the coil OR by pushing the magnet into the coil from the left-hand side OR by turning the magnet around and pulling it out of the left-hand side of the coil.
b)   By pushing the magnet in and immediately pulling it out again.
c)   By rapidly pushing the magnet in and out of the coil a number of times.
Q3   E.g. The cog wheel is attached to the bicycle wheel. The cog is attached to a magnet — as the wheel turns, the cog turns and rotates the magnet in a coil of wire on a soft iron core. This induces a potential difference in the coil and a current flows in the wire. The coil is connected in a circuit with the light bulb and so the bulb lights up.

Pages 94-97 — Transformers

Q1   1. A source of alternating potential difference is applied to the primary coil.
2. An alternating current flows in the primary coil.
3. This produces an alternating magnetic field in the iron core.
4. The magnetic field produced inside the secondary coil induces an alternating potential difference at the ends of the secondary coil.
5. If this is applied to an external circuit, an alternating current will flow in that circuit.
Q2 a)   When a current flows in the left-hand coil it generates a magnetic field which induces a current in the right hand coil and causes the needle of the ammeter to deflect. Since a current can only be induced when the magnetic field changes, the deflection only occurs when the current is switched on or off.

Physics 3b — Forces and Electromagnetism

b) You could put an iron core through the two coils / add more turns to the coils / add more cells to the battery etc. This would make the magnetic field stronger and therefore cause bigger deflections in the ammeter.

Q3 True, false, true.

Q4 A step-down transformer.

Q5 a) A transformer consists of an iron core and two coils.

b) Step-up transformers have more turns on the secondary coil than the primary coil.

c) In a step-down transformer the potential difference across the secondary coil is less than the potential difference across the primary coil.
OR
In a step-up transformer the potential difference across the secondary coil is greater than the potential difference across the primary coil.

Q6 a) The alternating current produces an alternating magnetic field in the core, which in turn induces an alternating potential difference in the secondary coil.

b) Only an alternating current can produce the constantly-changing magnetic field needed to continually induce a voltage in the secondary coil.

Q7 Ash is **wrong** because the iron core carries magnetic field, not current.

Q8 a) True, true, false, true.

b) E.g. any one from: mobile phone chargers / power supplies.

Q9 a) It is a step-down transformer — it reduces the voltage from 240 V to 12 V.

b) i) $P = V \times I = 240 \times 0.25 = $ **60 W.**

ii) $P = V \times I = 12 \times 5 = $ **60 W.**

c) Transformers are nearly 100% efficient.

Q10 The number of turns increases by a factor of 40 so the voltage will also increase by a factor of 40. So the input voltage would need to be 10 000 ÷ 40 = **250 V.**
Alternatively, use the equation:

$$\frac{V_p}{V_s} = \frac{N_p}{N_s}, \quad \frac{V_p}{10\,000} = \frac{100}{4000}, \quad V_p = \frac{10\,000 \times 100}{4000} = \textbf{250 V.}$$

Q11

Number of turns on primary coil	Voltage to primary coil (V)	Number of turns on secondary coil	Voltage to secondary coil (V)
1000	12	4000	**48**
1000	**10**	2000	20
1000	12	**1000**	12
71 739	33 000	500	230

Q12 a) Output voltage = 230 V × (8000/5000) = **368 V.**

b) 230 ÷ 20 = 11.5. So there must be 11.5 times more turns on the primary coil than on the secondary. Andy could either:
Keep 5000 turns on the primary coil and adapt the **secondary coil** to have 5000 ÷ 11.5 = **435 turns.**
OR
Keep 8000 turns on the secondary coil and adapt the **primary coil** to have 8000 × 11.5 = **92 000 turns.**

Q13 $V_p \times I_p = V_s \times I_s$
So, $I_p = (V_s \times I_s) \div V_p = $
$(110 \times 20) \div 230 = $ **9.6 A**

Pages 98-100 — Mixed Questions — Physics 3b

Q1 a) Anticlockwise moment = 1000 × 0.6 = 600 Nm
F = 600 ÷ 1.8 = **333 N**

b) The wheelbarrow was tilted so its **centre of mass** moved beyond the edge of its base. This caused a **resultant moment**, causing the wheelbarrow to tip.

c) E.g. the position of the centre of mass, width of the base.

Q2 a) f = 1 ÷ T = 1 ÷ 2 = **0.5 Hz**

b) The force applied to the water at the top of the bag is transmitted to water in other parts of the bag, and causes water to squirt out of the hole.

c) E.g. The large piston has a greater cross-sectional area than the small piston. A small force is applied to the small piston to create a pressure on a liquid. Pressure is transmitted equally through a liquid, so the pressure is the same at the large piston. F = P × A, so there will be a larger force at the larger piston.

Q3 a) The iron core increases the strength of the magnetic field produced by the current in the solenoid.

b) When the switch is closed the electromagnet is turned on, setting up a magnetic field. The iron rocker is attracted towards the electromagnet, so it pivots. This closes the contacts in the motor's circuit and turns the motor on.

Q4 a) The motion tells you which way the forces must be acting — see below.

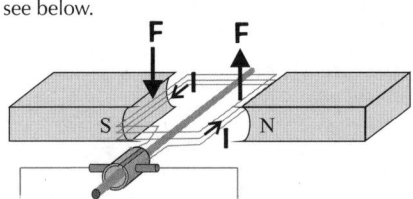

b) Use Fleming's Left-Hand Rule on one side of the coil. E.g. for the right-hand side of the coil, the field (first finger) goes from right to left (north to south), the motion (thumb) goes upwards, giving you the current (second finger) going into the page.

c) E.g. increase the current, use a stronger magnet.

Q5 a) An alternating potential difference is induced because the coil experiences a magnetic field which is changing (and 'cutting' through the coil).

b) The induced potential difference would be in the opposite direction (when the magnet is at any given position).

Q6 a) gravity

b) i) False

ii) False

c) A

Q7 a) Ratio of turns (secondary:primary) is 200:1000 = 1:5. So the output voltage will be 230 ÷ 5 = **46 V.**

b) i) Iron.

ii) It transfers the magnetic field from the primary to the secondary coil.

c) 33 kV = 33 000 V. Then:
Secondary voltage/Primary voltage = 230/33 000. So No. of turns on secondary coil = 2000 × 230 ÷ 33 000 = 14 turns.

d) E.g. they are lighter and smaller than traditional transformers and so are useful for lightweight devices like chargers. They are also more efficient, as they don't use much power when plugged in but have no load (i.e. a mobile phone) attached.

ISBN 978 1 84762 852 7

9 781847 628527

SAEA44

CGP

GCSE
Extension Science

Exam Board: AQA

Answer Book

Contents

Published by CGP

ISBN: 978 1 84762 852 7

www.cgpbooks.co.uk

Printed by Elanders Ltd, Newcastle upon Tyne.
Clipart from Corel®

Based on the classic CGP style created by Richard Parsons.